Writings of Toyohiko Kagawa

Upper Room Spiritual Classics®

Selected, edited, and introduced by
KEITH BEASLEY-TOPLIFFE

UPPER
ROOM BOOKS®
NASHVILLE

WRITINGS OF TOYOHIKO KAGAWA
Copyright © 1998 by Upper Room Books
Previously published as *Living Out Christ's Love: Selected Writings of Toyohiko Kagawa*
All rights reserved.

Upper Room Books' website: books.upperroom.org

Cover design: Tim Green | Faceout Studio
Interior design and typesetting: PerfecType, Nashville, TN

ISBN 978-0-8358-1652-6 (print) | ISBN 978-0-8358-1687-8 (mobi) | ISBN 978-0-8358-1688-5 (epub)

Library of Congress Cataloging-in-Publication Data

Kagawa, Toyohiko, 1888–1960.
   [Selections. English. 1998]
   Living out Christ's love: selected writings of Toyohiko Kagawa.
    p. cm.—(Upper Room spiritual classics. Series 2)
   ISBN 0-8358-0836-X
   1. Christian life—Meditations. 2. Kagawa, Toyohiko, 1888–1960. I. Title. II.
Series.
BV4501.2.K24213 1998
230—dc21
                                            97-35464
                                             CIP

Contents

Introduction

In the period between the First and Second World Wars, Toyohiko Kagawa was often mentioned together with Gandhi and Schweitzer as a model of how to blend prayer, personal caring, and social action. His conviction that the redeeming love of Christ on the cross should be not merely admired but imitated took him into the worst slums of Japan, but also into the emperor's palace. He personally took care of the poor, from starving babies to dying elders. He established settlement houses, worked for the formation of labor unions and peasant unions, carried on evangelistic campaigns, and served on various national relief committees.

Despite health problems that left him nearly blind, Kagawa wrote more than one hundred books. Many of them were bestsellers in Japan and were popular in English translation as well. In addition to writings on theology and Christian living, he published economic studies and several novels and collections of poetry.

Kagawa's popularity in the United States was hurt by anti-Japanese sentiment during World War II. During the Cold War, some Americans viewed his Christian socialism as too close to communism (though Kagawa regularly denounced Marxism). Today he is nearly forgotten in the United States.

He often stated that his evangelistic goal was to have a million Christians in Japan. In 1990, there were an estimated 1,075,000.

Kagawa's World

At the end of the nineteenth century, Japan was just emerging from a two-and-a-half-century attempt to keep out Western civilization and influence. The first Portuguese traders had come to Japan in 1543, followed by Dutch and English. After an uprising in 1637, Japan was closed to the West except for a few Dutch traders allowed to visit one port. Though a few embassies were established in the 1850s, the isolation did not end until the reestablishment of imperial rule in 1867.

Though the feudal system was officially abolished with the 1889 constitution, most of the wealth was still held by a few families. Most farmland was owned by wealthy individuals and farmed by tenants. Peasant farmers also formed the source of cheap labor for the growing factories. Slums grew rapidly in major cities. One of the worst was the Shinkawa in Kobe, where eleven thousand people lived in eleven city blocks, often several sharing a "house" only six feet square.

Meanwhile, Japan was steadily expanding its territory through military action. It won Formosa (Taiwan) and part of Manchuria from China in 1895 and half of Sakhalin Island from Russia in 1905 (a war protested by new Christian and college student Kagawa). Japan annexed Korea in 1910 and Manchuria in 1931 with constant war against China from that point on. The expansion ended with the defeat of Japan in World War II and all but the home islands was lost.

Three religious traditions coexisted (and still coexist) in Japan, not simply side by side, but intertwined in people's lives. Shinto is the ancient religion of Japan. It is primarily a way of devotion to many local gods. In fact, the name Shinto comes from the Chinese words *shen tao*, "the way of good spirits." In addition to personal acts of devotion, there are major festivals at various times. But this devotion is largely divorced from morality.

Confucianism came to Japan from China in the fifth century. Originally a philosophical system taught by Master Kung (Kung Fu-tse, 551–479 BCE), Confucianism focused on personal and social relationships, especially those between father and son, husband and wife, older brother and younger brother, older friend and younger friend, and ruler and subject. Each role is characterized by a particular attitude; for instance, love in the father and filial piety in the son (attitudes that Kagawa could point to in the Father and Son of Christianity). Confucianism also brought along the ancient Chinese tradition of ancestor worship.

Buddhism was another imported religion, coming from India by way of China and Korea in the seventh century. The

Buddha (Siddhartha Gautama, 563–483 BCE) taught that suffering is universal and is caused by selfish desire, which can be eliminated by following the eightfold path of right knowledge, intention, speech, conduct, means of livelihood, effort, mindfulness, and concentration. By the time Buddhism reached Japan, Buddha was being worshiped, and there was a strong emphasis on achieving mindfulness and concentration through prayer, either the repetition of short formulas or the silent emptiness of Zen.

These three traditions were seen as complementary, not contradictory. People were presented at Shinto shrines at birth and took part in Shinto rituals, sought enlightenment through Buddhist practices, and conducted their personal relationships according to the teaching of Confucius until they were buried with Confucian rites.

Christianity first came to Japan with the Portuguese traders. Jesuit missionary Francis Xavier arrived in 1549 and Christianity enjoyed modest success. The other traditions could easily accommodate Christ as an enlightened master. But when missionaries insisted that only Christ was right and all other traditions had no truth at all, anti-Christian feeling grew. In 1614, missionaries were ordered to leave the country and Christianity was suppressed. At least three thousand Christians were martyred by 1637 when contact with the West was cut off. For two and a half centuries Christianity continued underground. In 1865, when they felt it was safe to reveal themselves, there were about sixty thousand *Kakure Kirishitan* or "hidden Christians." The 1889 constitution offered religious freedom "within limits not prejudicial to peace and not antagonistic to duties as citizens."

Kagawa's Life

Toyohiko Kagawa was born July 10, 1888, in Kobe, Japan. His father, Junichi, was married to the only child of the head of the Kagawa family and then adopted as the heir to the family fortune. The marriage was childless, and Junichi abandoned his wife to live with a geisha named Kame. Toyohiko was the fourth of their five children. Junichi adopted these children to make them his legal heirs. When Toyohiko was four, his father died, followed two months later by his mother. He went to live with his father's wife and her mother on the Kagawa estate, where he was tolerated but not loved. Later he lived with an uncle who paid for his schooling.

In 1903, Kagawa decided to learn English and found instruction at a Christian school run by missionaries, Dr. C. A. Logan and Dr. H. W. Myers. He learned English from the Bible and read about a Father who would love him unconditionally. He was baptized on February 14, 1904. When he decided to become a Christian minister, his uncle disinherited him. Soon after entering seminary he began to preach in the slums of Kobe. Tuberculosis sent him to a fishing village to recover for most of a year. When he returned to seminary, he determined to live in the slums among the poorest people. He moved into the Shinkawa on Christmas 1909. In addition to continuing his studies, doing relief work, and preaching, he published his first books. A young woman factory worker named Haru came to see what he was doing and stayed to help him. She became a Christian and married him in 1913. They eventually had three children.

In 1914, Kagawa went to Princeton Theological Seminary and graduated in 1916 with a Bachelor of Divinity. Haru stayed behind to carry on his work until he returned in 1917. Kagawa began to work on the roots of poverty. Beginning with a dock workers' strike in 1921, he helped organize labor and farmers' unions, and was jailed for those activities. He made a lecture tour of the United States and Europe in 1924, the first of many such trips. In 1938, while in India for a World Missionary Council, he met Mahatmas Gandhi. He opposed the growing militarism in Japan and was jailed again in 1940. In 1941 he went to the United States to try to maintain peace. During the war he was either in prison or living in exile at a sanitarium on a small island. As the war ended, he was asked to work on relief of refugees and became an adviser to the prime minister. Later, he helped organize a Socialist Political Party. In 1950 he again toured the United States and began to work for a strong United Nations, which he hoped could become a world government. He died in Tokyo on April 25, 1960.

Further Reading

Most English translations of Kagawa's books are out of print. The exception is a collection of daily meditations. There are several biographies of Kagawa in English. The most recent, *Toyohiko Kagawa*, is by Robert Schildgen (Centenary Press, 1988).

Kagawa himself read very broadly. He frequently refers to the life and works of John Wesley and the life of Francis of Assisi. He also translated the works of Albert Schweitzer into Japanese.

Note on the Text

These selections come from a variety of Kagawa's works and several translators. They have been edited for length and inclusive language, with a few adjustments in punctuation and spelling. Kagawa often freely paraphrases scripture. More exact quotes have been conformed to the New Revised Standard Version.

Kagawa's Testimony

From *Unconquerable Kagawa*, Part II, Chapter II,
"An Awakened Kagawa"

In 1950, Kagawa made a speaking tour of the United States. He often told parts of his own story. Friends compiled these parts into a brief autobiography from transcripts of his talks. Here are selections from the early part of Kagawa's life, beginning when he was about fifteen.

One day I was walking down the street and there was a tent. Hymn singing was coming from the inside. It was a vacation Bible school. I went in. Dr. C. A. Logan, an American missionary from Virginia, was preaching. He was telling about love and the many sacrifices Christ made for all humankind, and it brought joy into my heart.

Dr. Logan introduced me to Dr. H. W. Myers, and I went to him to study English. He said to me: "Mr. Kagawa, I am willing to help you study English, but it will help if you memorize a few verses from the Sermon on the Mount." When I began to study these wonderful verses from the Sermon on the Mount, I discovered that the Creator of the universe is my

Father in heaven. Being an orphan, I discovered that God is my Father. Oh, I was happy!

When I read these verses, life took on new meaning, and the flowers everywhere seemed to blossom. I knew that what I read was true, so in secret I began to pray to God.

At that time I had gone to live with my uncle. He said to me: "Toyohiko, you may study English with that American missionary, but don't believe in Christianity. It is a bad religion. About three hundred years ago it tried to capture Japan. You must not believe in Christianity."

But I thought he was making a mistake, because Buddhism couldn't make me a good boy, nor Shintoism, nor Confucian teaching. But since I had begun to pray to the Father in heaven in the name of Jesus Christ, I felt new strength coming to my life. So I would retire to my bedroom, and putting the bedcovers over my head, I would simply pray: "O God, make me a good boy! Amen." I did not go to church. If I had gone to church, I would have been kicked out of my house, which I wouldn't have liked. So I stayed away from church.

About eight months passed. I went to the American missionary to borrow some books. He asked me many questions: "Mr. Kagawa, do you believe in Christ?" "Yes sir." "Do you pray to God?" "Yes sir." "How do you pray to God?" I hesitated a minute, but then I answered, "Under the bedcovers, sir." He looked at me and said, "Why don't you come to church?" I told him if I would do so, I should be kicked out of my house, which I wouldn't like. Then he said to me, "Mr. Kagawa, you are a timid and cowardly boy." Now all Japanese boys hate the word *coward*. So I said, "You had better repeat the word *coward* once more." "You are a timid and cowardly boy," he said. Then I told him that if he would keep on repeating the word *coward* I would go to church.

I did go to church, and on the third Sunday after I started, when I was fifteen years old, I was baptized. Oh, I was glad and happy! In appearance I was a monkey, but inside I was a son of God!

When I finished high school, I determined to be a minister for Christ. I had to leave my house, and I was disinherited because my uncle didn't like it, but Dr. Myers put me in the Presbyterian college in Tokyo.

After two years at college, when I was nineteen, I spent the summer preaching in the slums. There I preached continuously by myself on the streets every day for forty days.

On the fortieth day, at about nine o'clock in the evening, it began to rain while I was still preaching. For a week my voice had been getting weaker, and when the rain began falling, my body was swaying to and fro. At one time I had difficulty in getting my breath. I began to feel horribly cold, but I determined, whatever happened, to finish my sermon.

"In conclusion," I cried, "I tell you God is love, and I will affirm God's love till I fall. Where there is love, God and life reveal themselves."

My fever was so high that I actually felt I would collapse. Somehow I stumbled back to where I was staying and went to bed. For two days I lay there coughing worse and worse, spitting up blood, but with no money to call a doctor.

At the end of the second day the pastor of the church did send for a doctor. He examined me. He told me that I had tubercular pneumonia, and there was no hope of my recovery.

On the third day my condition seemed completely hopeless. I could not cough any more or even breathe without effort. For a week I lay there, just praying and waiting. Then the hemorrhages got worse and I got a very high fever. I thought that the time had come for me to die. The doctor said to notify my friends.

The sun was setting in the west. I could see its reflection on my pillow. For four hours I prayed, waiting for my last breath. Then there came a peculiar, mysterious experience; an ecstatic consciousness of God; a feeling that God was inside me and all around me. I felt a great ecstasy and joy. I coughed up a cupful of clotted blood. I could breathe again. The fever was reduced. I forgot to die. The doctor came back at nine-thirty. He was disappointed. He had written a certificate for my cremation and feared the people would call him a quack.

For a month I rested, praying and reading and meditating. Then I returned to school—this time to the Kobe Theological Seminary. I set forth at once to preach on the street corners of Shinkawa, the worst slum district in Japan. I was able to preach for a whole week before my strength gave out again.

This time the doctor seemed to think it was really serious, so Dr. Myers put me in a hospital for four months. I didn't want to bother him so much, so I left the hospital. I had only fifteen yen, but I rented a small fishing man's cottage for one yen a month. In your money that was only fifty cents. There was not much of anything in that cottage—no cot, no mattress—so I got some straw to make a bed on the floor and I lived in that house nearly a year.

People didn't like to get close to me because of my terrible disease, so I was very lonesome. Then came Dr. Myers. He had taken his vacation and left his wife to come visit me. He stayed in that cottage about four days. We slept in the same bed. I asked if he wasn't afraid of me. "Your disease is contagious," he said, "but love is more contagious."

At that moment I realized more truly than ever what love really means: that love can have no fear; that love can have no limits; that love encompasses everything—the people sick like me, and the people sick in spirit and mind. I thought I must love everybody, too—even the horrible people in the slums. I decided I must not be sick any more. I told God that if He would let me live, I would serve His children in the slums. Pretty soon I began to get well again.

Stories from the Slums

From *Unconquerable Kagawa*, Part II, Chapter II,
"An Awakened Kagawa"

Kagawa's first days in the Shinkawa slum of Kobe set the tone for much of his ministry there. Here are several stories from those early days, compiled from his talks forty years later.

As soon as I returned to school, I went back to preach on the street corners of Shinkawa. One night before Christmas I was preaching and there came an ex-convict. When he was born, his mother did not like him, so she threw him on the ground and tried to kill him, but he didn't die. Instead he lived and became a thief. He had a technique. He would set fire to a place. All the neighbors would run to the house. Then he would enter the other houses and steal. Once two hundred houses burned down. He was put in prison for nine years. While he was there he got the New Testament from a pick-pocket. He was converted and he said, "Mr. Kagawa, there is a vacant house in Shinkawa."

The house had been vacant for many years because in that house a certain laborer had been killed and some said a ghost was there. Because of the ghost the rent was very cheap—only two yen a month. So on Christmas 1909, I moved into the haunted house. I made my own bed on the very spot where the man had been killed. To my disappointment the ghost didn't come. I was a hero because I lived in the house that was haunted by a ghost. Everyone said I was courageous. People said I had some supernatural power that drove away the ghost.

In Shinkawa there were eleven thousand people crowded into eleven verminous, unpaved alleys. My house had two rooms, the front one six feet wide by nine feet long and the back one six feet square. It had no windows, and light and air came in through the door. Outside there were a community kitchen, a water hydrant, and a common toilet to serve the needs of about twenty families. The place was filthy and full of disease. It smelled horrible. All sorts of people lived there—scavengers, freight handlers, day laborers, factory workers, garbage collectors, vendors, cargo carriers, fortune-tellers, gamblers, beggars, thieves, drunks, murderers, and prostitutes. I discovered as many as eight hundred ex-convicts living there and a hundred and fifty girls living as prostitutes.

The next day after I moved there a man came to me and said, "I am out of employment so please let me stay with you." His nickname was Mr. Statue because he had nothing to do but to stand still on the corner. So Mr. Statue came and stayed with me. I slept with him and got his skin disease. I would get up very early. Mr. Statue didn't get up at all. I asked him why he remained in bed. He said, "Mr. Kagawa, I need some surplus energy." Then he said, "Since I have no food to eat, if I remain in bed I will not waste my energy."

A few days later a second man came. He had just been released from jail. He had been selling his wares when a young man upset his basket and destroyed all the bean pods. He was instinctively angry and knocked the young man down. The young man was killed instantly. The judge had sympathy for the murderer, however, and kept him under arrest for only eighteen months. When he came to me, he was suffering from a mental disease. Every night he dreamed there was a ghost. He came to me and said, "Mr. Kagawa, you have some sort of supernatural power to drive away ghosts. I dream every night there is a ghost. Please let me grasp your hand. Some mysterious power will flow into my body from yours, and I will not dream about the ghost." So I let him grasp my hand. He dreamed about a ghost and he cried out in the middle of the night. He screamed. It sounded terrible. He remained about four years with me and recovered from the mental disease.

Then there came a third man. He was suffering from syphilis. His neck was covered with sores. He looked terrible, but I took him in. I had only my monthly scholarship of eleven yen from the theological seminary. That was $5.50. It was impossible to feed four people on eleven yen even in Japan, so I went to work cleaning chimneys and in this way earned another

$5.00 a month. But even that was not enough, so we passed up lunch and had only two meals a day. We put water into the rice and we watered our stomachs. I couldn't work hard at all. I was hungry. "Give us this day our daily bread." If you have plenty of food, you can never understand the meaning of the Lord's Prayer.

A Christian nurse found out about us and gave me five yen. I was glad, so I said to Mr. Statue, "Let us make some good rice." We boiled the rice hard and had three meals. They were delicious.

Once a beggar came to me and said, "You are a Christian, so give me your shirt." I had to give it to him. Then he demanded my coat and trousers. I had to give him those, too. I then had no clothes. A woman who lived nearby, a reformed prostitute, gave me a kimono. It had a bright red lining and the people laughed at me. They called me a fool. I agreed, but said that I was "Christ's fool."

There was a woman who was the wife of a wicked pirate. She had no money to feed her baby only a hundred days old, so she was just letting it starve. I began to give her condensed milk for the baby. A few weeks later she disappeared. The following July in the hot weather I was suddenly called to appear in the police court. The chief of police said, "You are Mr. Kagawa?" "Yes," I said. "You have a wife?" "No." "You have a baby?" "No." "You had better confess you have a baby." "No, I have no baby. I am a bachelor." "You had better go see." I went to the prison cell and found that wicked woman with her baby that she said was mine. The woman was to be imprisoned for four years, but a baby cannot remain in prison in Japan. I took the baby and so this time became a mother. The baby had a high fever and almost died from the heat. It screamed and cried. I didn't know how to make milk from condensed milk. I went to the doctor and asked him how. I was just in the middle of examinations at the theological seminary. The baby started crying at midnight. Mr. Statue didn't move. He suffered from a mental disease. So I got up and fed the baby. I washed out its clothes. I sang it to sleep. Now I have a lot of sympathy for a mother. We cared for that baby about six months until we found a real mother. We didn't give it back to that woman.

When Tears Are Mingled

From *Songs from the Slums*

*Kagawa wrote of his experiences in the Shinkawa in novels (*Crossing the Death Line *and* A Shooter at the Sun) *and in several books of poetry. Lois J. Erickson translated some of these poems into English in 1935 as* Songs from the Slums. *The following poem is based on the last story in the preceding selection.*

Dawn coming in through the grayness
Lights up the place where she lies;
I am sodden with sleep, but I waken
At my starveling's fretful cries.

She is here on the floor beside me
   Wrapped in rags that stink;
     I change them;
   I hold her to feed her,
And sob as she struggles to drink.

Three days have I now been a woman,
With a mother's heart in my breast;

Do I doze but an hour
    Then she whimpers,
And I spring to soothe her to rest.

  Thin little dirty baby,
Wailing with pain all the while,
But I taste the bliss that no life should miss
When I look in her eyes and smile!

    Ah, she is ill
      Little Ishi,
  Life has abused her so;
Safe from the fiend who had meant to kill,
  Fever has laid her low.

Through the night I labored to save her;
  We two were all alone.
Sharp in the fearful stillness
The neighbor's clock struck one.

Then walls went creaking, creaking,
  Blackened timbers groaned.
In this house by murder haunted,
The low-hung ceilings moaned.

Boards in the floor beneath us
Which have sucked blood, warm and bright

Held their breath and shrieked of death
    Into the ghostly night. . . .

    Why is the world so cruel?
    Seen with Ishi's eyes,
    The earth, and all things in it
    Is a mountain-pile of ice.

    Then do you pity Ishi?
    I need your pity, too.
    I must help; I must help,
        But am helpless.

    Oh, to be taught what to do!
    Men are consoled by their women,
    But this scrap in my tired arm lies,
    A shriveled doll from the junk-heap,
    And the strong man who holds her cries.

    Why are you quiet, Ishi?
    Why are your eyes shut, why?
    Wait, oh wait, little sick one,
    It is too soon to die.
    Think of my struggle to save you,
    Will you not stay with me?
    Listen; Death shall not take you;
    I have no burial fee!

(How now?
Through the daze of this dreadful plight
Do I wince at a bedbug's filthy bite?)

Cry again, little Ishi;
Cry once more, once more;
What will it take to make you wake?
For I cannot let you go!

I call; but you do not hear me;
I clasp you; you do not move.
It is not to pain I would bring you again,
There is Love in the world; there is Love!

Will she not cry?
I shall make her;
Here in my close embrace
I kiss her wan lips growing grayer;
My drawn face touches her face.
Fast are my frightened tears flowing,
Falling on Ishi's eyes;
With her cold, still tears they are mingled,
O God . . . at last . . . she cries!

The Healing Power of God

From *New Life through God*, Chapter I,
"New Life through God"

In the late 1920s, Kagawa was speaking frequently at evangelistic rallies throughout Japan. Some of these talks were taken down by followers and published. Elizabeth Kilburn translated them as New Life Through God. *Here Kagawa speaks about God's healing power from his own experiences.*

The fullness of God's power in the universe is wonderful. Even in illness, there is a healing process. The mentally ill may be cured; there is peace for those who are worried; and there is forgiveness for sinners. That is to say, there is a wonderful regenerating power, as well as a creative power, in the universe. And the way to find out about this power is through religion. The injured recover; even though bleeding, they become well. Even those with lung trouble may get well. The sick can be healed.

All my life I have been ill. While in the second year of middle school, I had to stop because the apex of one lung had become tubercular. I began to have hemorrhages when I was seventeen years old, and two years later I was so seriously ill that I had to rest for a year. For four or five years the fever did not leave me. At twenty I hardly weighed seventy-six pounds; I now weigh more than one hundred and forty. So when you are told that you have tuberculosis, you need not worry. Sickness has to do with the spirit. When the spirit is healed, the physical sickness will go. If you say, "I have consumption, therefore it's hopeless," you will not get well. I now have diabetes, and I have had severe attacks of pleurisy. Because of another trouble, I cannot eat solid food. My heart is weak, too, and since I caught trachoma in the slums a film has formed over the cornea, injuring my eyesight. The doctor has said over and over that I could not recover; but because I believed I would, I did. When an auto that I was in collided with an electric train, I injured my spine and broke my arm. At the time of the great earthquake of 1927, I went to the town of Ayabe, in the province of Tango, and there suffered from inflammation of the middle ear. With all these ailments, I am still active. Illness is a matter of the spirit. I feel that it is half mental and half physical. If you believe, come what may, you can overcome it and recover. This is religion. I have peace because my heart is easy. I have crossed the death-line, so nothing matters. Since I have as good as died once, the rest is all gain. What is living of me is merely the spirit.

If, without worry, you can feel that you can put yourself in God's hands and become free, you will get well. Tuberculosis is an internal injury of the body. If you injure the outside of the body, even though the blood flow, you will get well. So why not believe that an internal injury may be cured, also? If you do not recover, it is because you think you will not. We must conquer illness. Surely we believe that God is with us; that is faith. We do not get well by taking the doctor's medicine only. The regenerating power of the God of heaven, helping as it works through a person, is the real doctor. The human doctor is like the midwife, an assistant. We must wait for God's healing power. It is the same with the mind. It is said that insanity in many forms is incurable; but when the spirit becomes quiet, the insane recover. Even things that are said to be incurable are curable. Insanity is recessive; out of four children it may be that only one will be afflicted, and in four or five generations the strain may disappear, never to return.

When we think of this, we realize that the universe is very wonderful, and not a haphazard affair. People make it topsy-turvy. Confusion is brought about by syphilis and alcohol. Much of the insanity comes from them. If we do not get rid of syphilis and alcohol, we shall not get rid of mental diseases. A great majority of the feeble-minded and epileptic children born into the world are a result of drinking sake. A man just out of prison, who had no one to look after him, came to my house for shelter. I received him. He had had no sake for four months, so he asked for some spending money. I gave it to him, but when he wanted it regularly, I refused. At that he grew violent and broke four of my front teeth. That man was frenzied by drink, crazed with the thirst for drink. There are many such in Japan. The father of a professor in a medical college in Osaka was a drunkard. He abused his wife and also his little son so that the son, who was a teacher, could not stand it. One day the father actually strangled the mother to death. He was charged with manslaughter. In the meantime, the son hanged himself in the warehouse. There are many tragedies like that. The responsibility for them is human, not divine. Even so, the God of heaven endeavors to lessen the bad effects of human sin, for though the grandfather may be badly affected, very often the grandson may be only slightly so. Fortunately, in heaven there is healing power.

The Lord's Prayer

From *New Life through God*, Chapter VI,
"God and Prayer"

The Lord's Prayer is central to Kagawa. He often refers to some part of it. In this selection he systematically comments on the entire prayer.

The Lord's Prayer is most beautiful. We cannot go beyond this in prayer. We may analyze it thus:

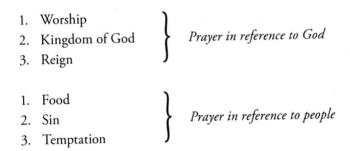

1. Worship
2. Kingdom of God   *Prayer in reference to God*
3. Reign

1. Food
2. Sin   *Prayer in reference to people*
3. Temptation

The first part of the prayer pertains to the essence of God. The first things we, as human beings, must do are to throw out all selfishness and be willing to be whatever God sees fit.

Worship is absolute devotion. It means perfect trust. God gives us our mission in life. Because we are born in order to reveal the glory of God, we must overcome selfish desires, and pray that we may become ornaments of some kind for God. One becomes the jewel in the crown, another some hidden but useful part of the robe or crown. But each has a definite mission. Who knows but some people may be born to become the hair of the head! If, however, it is distasteful to be the hair, and the hair should all drop out, how funny that would be. We must all be uncomplaining, for all cannot be the jewels of the crown. Some may have to be the nails. But anyway nails are ornaments. Only as we worship in this spirit can we really pray.

Next we must pray for God's kingdom. We must pray that we may realize the kingdom of God in society; but we cannot do this by being hermits. Not only must we work to make Japan God's kingdom, or just to make China better; the whole world must become God's kingdom. We must pray not for a kingdom that can be found on the map, but for an eternal kingdom of God. The kingdom of God is a problem of the heart. When the time is ripe, it will come to pass. Therefore at all times we must pray that the reign of God should continue. In this, both time and space are included. We desire that God's eternal reign may last throughout history. We must pray that God's wind may always, eternally blow, not only as during the Mongolian invasion, but at all times.

There is a time, however, when God loses hope for us; that is when the Holy Spirit leaves us. When we lie and call evil good and good evil, the Holy Spirit leaves us. Among the five hundred *Lohar* of Buddhism, one represents "perversity." That means when things on the bottom come to be on the top, low things become high, the value is reversed, good and evil are turned around, and crime becomes the ideal thing to do. Jesus prayed that God would not leave us in our sins, but save us.

Jesus, praying about food, said, *Give us this day our daily bread.* Therefore it is not a mistake to pray for physical needs. We cannot say that when we pray, "Give me work," or "Give me a home," God will not give it to us. I have had much experience in having such prayers answered.

When you are living in the slums, many come, saying, "Give, give." Once I had no money and was in great trouble, having given lodging to sixteen sick people. At that time I prayed, "God, I have sixteen people lying here, and I have no money! I cannot give them food to eat. O God, give me two yen today." That very day I received five yen from someone. I have had that kind of experience many times. When many are in trouble, we cannot help but pray, not for ourselves, but for them. When Elijah, who opposed the oppression of Israel, prayed that the rain and dew would be dried up, the rain stopped. During the three years that Elijah was living by the river Cherith, ravens brought him food. The strange thing is that when we walk the straight path, "a raven" will be sent to help. If there are those who do not believe it, just look at my work. I work as hard as I can, but one person alone could not possibly help all the laboring classes. The work would be a failure unless thousands, yes, tens of thousands of "ravens" came to help. Our prayers are answered through gifts of bread and money. That is an experienced fact.

Furthermore, we must forgive one another's sin. Even though there is sin that others do not know about, it is forgiven. Jesus forgave such sin as he died on the cross. Of course, it is not right to think that because we are forgiven it is all right to sin, but if we ask for pardon before God, we are surely forgiven. For that purpose Jesus himself was nailed to the cross.

Next we must pray about "temptations" or trials. In the Roman age the Christians were so harried and anxious, they did not know what to do. At that time the prayer that they might be saved from persecution came naturally to their lips. Surely God will hear those who pray that they may be saved from the persecution that is sure to come, and be taken out of the hurricane and whirlwind. Jesus said, "Pray then in this way." In the Lord's Prayer the first sentence in reference to God (worship) and the first in reference to humankind (bread) are connected. The second in reference to God (kingdom of God) and the second in reference to humankind (sin), have relation to each other. The third pair, "reign" and "temptation," are somewhat related. We ask for bread for our daily living, and that for love's sake our sin may be forgiven so that the reign of

God's kingdom may come to pass. We cannot use or invent a prayer more complete than this one. This, the Lord's Prayer, is our model.

Because Jesus taught us this prayer, for many thousands of years it will still be prayed. And during these years many hundreds of thousands, yes, billions of people will have used it! And we will come to believe that prayer is answered. This is not mere theory. It is wonderful how happy we become when we pray. Just merely worshiping God, without any special petition, is prayer. It is filial piety just to say, "Good morning," to your father. "Father, I thank you for this beautiful weather" is prayer. Prayer is not merely petition, but is coming face-to-face with God; not merely asking, but praise and thanksgiving, too. To think that we must have a priest to make our prayers is a mistake. To say, "O God, the weather is fine," even that is all right! It is not necessary to pray like this, but it is also not necessary to use difficult classical expressions. If we just talk as we would to our human father, it is enough. For a little child to say, "Thank you, God. Amen," is all right.

God's Love in Our Lives

From *New Life through God*, Chapter IX,
"God and Daily Living"

One of Kagawa's constant themes is the importance of living out our faith from day to day.

There is a human inclination to seek God in the individual life, but the attempt to realize God in social living is rare. For this reason the Christian religion is sometimes thought to be an amusement for the leisure classes, for the trifling bourgeoisie, or confined to the hermit or ascetic. But religion is not that. John Fiske, in defining religion, said that religion is God working among people in everyday living. True religion is that which not only looks toward heaven, but also turns toward earth with a feeling of being in heaven.

Victor Hugo said, "Religion must be followed by all types of people. When we walk on the ground, one foot is always lifted and the other one adheres to the earth." A person would never become discouraged who felt this way. Forgetting the nature of religious experience, we live assiduously for earthly things only. When one foot is lifted and one foot is on earth, the real nature of religious experience is revealed: we walk and go forward.

Jesus was a carpenter, but in the midst of that simple life he revealed God to people. He was born in a manger in a stable. His parents walked about looking for a place to stay, but found them all filled up, so there was nothing to do but go into a stable. There the baby was born. The image of God, however, resided in the child. This one humble laborer has moved the world! Herein lies the realization of religion. Many think while they hold the throttle or the rudder, God is not near or needed. "While we are praying, God is near; but while we are working, God is not," they say. It is a mistake to think that although God is present in church, God is not present when we are making bean mash. We cannot call anything true religion unless through it God may be found at the counter, in the kitchen, or in the shop. Jesus Christ revealed the image of God to the world, and his religion was in his everyday living. The Christian religion includes not only his teachings and ideals, but also his daily life.

Many are mistaken in that, although they want to believe in religion, they think that they must learn philosophy first. After studying philosophy for five or six years, they come to understand it; but it is too late, for in the meantime life has gone on, and they are a few years behind. For us to think of reasoning alone will not do; yet that is what many young people do. Some young people say, "After finishing six hundred pages of this book, I'll be religious." But we living human beings must have a living religion. We understand religion for the first time when we experiment with living things.

This is a religion of life. True religion is not that of books. We must experience religion while traveling, while eating our meals, and while working. In the Bible it is written that Jesus was charged with being overfond of eating. Jesus ate so much that the Pharisees asked his disciples, "Doesn't your Master ever fast?" Jesus answered, "Can we fast on the wedding night?" We fast at a funeral, but when God and humanity are married—at a happy occasion like this—we do not fast. This is the realization of religion.

Jesus, furthermore, always remained a laborer. He worked as a carpenter until he was thirty years of age, and during his three-year ministry he worked hard. Even on his holidays he helped people and healed the sick. For that reason some people came to Jesus and asked, "Don't you rest even on a rest day?" "No, God always works; if God rested, the world would fall; therefore, while God works, I work also." According to Christ, therefore, daily living was religion.

Because Jesus was merciful and sympathetic, he served beggars, healed people with leprosy, raised the dead, opened the eyes of people who were blind, healed those with epilepsy or convulsions, and relieved those possessed with evil spirits, like those people whom we call "possessed by a badger or a fox." He also listened to the complaints of cross-examiners and the appeal of adulterers. He gave to ex-convicts and poor people and worked for their salvation. He always sympathized with the oppressed classes. So in this way he revived all kinds of people physiologically, psychologically, socially, and religiously. In Christ's activity itself may be seen the image of God. Because Jesus applied religion to life, this Christian religion has lasted up to the present day. God reveals *love*. Here may be seen the unspeakable happiness of life.

Seven Last Words

From *New Life through God*, Chapter IX,
"God and Daily Living"

Kagawa comments on Jesus' seven sayings from the cross in several of his books. To him, they show the persistence of love even in the face of death.

As Jesus was being crucified he spoke seven memorable sentences. They are known as "the seven words from the cross." While they were nailing his hands and feet to the cross, he said the first: "Father, forgive them—forgive those who are nailing me to the cross." That was not an easy thing to say. Tradition has it that Sogoro Sakura, as he was being crucified, died resentfully, saying, "Curses be upon you and your house to the eighth generation." And during eight generations, the Hotta family was cursed. It is most difficult to ask forgiveness for unreasonable people. This spirit comes from religious experience. We cannot do this without living the right kind of life. It was wonderful how Jesus could love the people who crucified him. He was able to do that because he had the great heart of God.

Tolstoy said that Jesus' Sermon on the Mount was his greatest teaching, but Confucius and Mo Ti and Buddha also taught some of the ideals of the Sermon on the Mount. That they could do, but not one of them prayed as Jesus did for the forgiveness of his enemies and slayers.

There were two robbers hanging, one on each side of Jesus. One of them, up to the very end, did not repent, but the other one extolled Jesus and said, "Remember me when you come into your kingdom," and Jesus answered, "Today you will be with me in Paradise." There are these two types of bad men in the world. One is absolutely unashamed of his evil conduct, like the robber who said, "Ah, Jesus, you have at last been hung up!" He had time to say even worse things as he was hanging there. The other robber, turning to the first one, said, "You be quiet. You are a bandit; it is all right for you to be crucified, but it is different with this just man." Then turning to Christ, he asked that he be remembered when Jesus came into his kingdom. Jesus answered with strong assurance. If we were to die now, would it be possible for us to use such words, I wonder? If someone asks us for something when we are suffering violent pain, we do not want to give it; we do not even want to talk. As soon as the request was made, Jesus answered, "All right." Up to the moment of his death Jesus had the will to save. In other words, he was actually living his religion even while he was dying. If he had not had the desire to save, he would not have given that answer.

He was worried about his mother. At the foot of the cross there were three women and one man. The women were Jesus' mother, Mary Magdalene, and his mother's younger sister; the man was the disciple, John. To his mother he said, "Rely on my disciple, John," and to John he said, "Take care of my mother." Jesus had filial piety, strong even in death.

The fourth thing that he said was, "I am thirsty." Four soldiers were standing there; one of them put an opiate up to his mouth, but he would not drink it. There are very few people who, passing through suffering, are in their right minds up to the very end. But Jesus, right up to the last, suffered for people and refused the drug.

Jesus' next words were, "My God, my God, why have you forsaken me?" Some people think that it was a wail, but that is not true. It is Psalm 22:1. He sang this in a loud voice. Some of those who heard it said that he was calling for Elijah. Jesus' death was prophesied many hundred years earlier. He died, feeling that the prophecy was being fulfilled. So the sixth time he spoke he said, "It is finished."

Jesus was different from other people. Not once during his lifetime did he say, "I am the Christ." In 1907, the year General Booth came to Japan, Mr. Toranosuke Miyazaki went around saying, "I am a Buddha; I am a Christ." Jesus, however, said not one word to that effect. He did not just talk with the mouth, but he suffered absolute agony, shedding his own blood for the salvation of people. He only accomplished his mission fully when he shed his blood, so he said, "It [my mission] is finished."

Then he spoke the seventh time, his last word: "Father, into your hands I commend my spirit." And so, through his death, as it were, apologizing to God for all sin, he breathed his last. That was at three o'clock on that same afternoon. When I was in the hospital for consumptives, a man named Nishimura was there. Every night before going to sleep he wrote up his diary and tidied up his desk, so he was "always ready to go to God," as he put it. He died as beautifully as though he were going to sleep.

Can we, like Christ, entrust our souls to God? Jesus' whole life is expressed in the Cross. The Cross is a practical experience of religion in daily life. When we have this actual living experience, then religion enters daily life. We must ever have this spirit.

True Success

From *The Religion of Jesus,* Chapter II,
"Jesus and Our Failures"

The Religion of Jesus (English translation by Helen F. Topping, 1931) is a series of meditations on various aspects of Jesus' life. Here Kagawa looks at Jesus as a failure who can therefore reach out to us when we fail.

Jesus Christ was crucified as a failure, and his disciples all ran away from him. Nevertheless, Jesus Christ did not call himself defeated. Jesus was a success, though apparently a failure. There are many who think themselves successful but do not realize that actually they are failures.

Once I visited the home of a shipping millionaire with the chief editor of the Osaka newspaper. When I went to that house, I asked the editor, "What will the owner do with this house?" He replied, "He will confine himself in it!" At that time I was living in a house six feet square and found it quite comfortable. When Kropotkin was in prison, he walked five miles a day in his cell. When I was put in the Tachibana prison in Kobe, I followed Kropotkin's example. My cell was about six feet square, and I could walk about six steps. I walked in the cell for about two miles every day. Thus I could think of my residence as being two miles wide! The writer of the epistle to the Hebrews could say, "Be content with what you have; for [God] has said, 'I will never leave you or forsake you.'" Saint Paul wrote from prison, "I have learned to be content with whatever I have."

Jesus Christ spent his life in destitution and had nothing to the last moment. Yet the Crucified One was the most successful person who ever lived. True success is to succeed in, to inherit, life. The truly successful person is the one who can enjoy the life of God. So long as you suffer because of crucifixion, destitution, or persecution, you can do nothing.

I know a young man in the slums who gets up at five in the morning, studies till six, and then goes out to work in the enamel factory all day long. When he comes back in the evening, he goes out to preach on the street every evening. He had no time he could call his own and continued this program for four years, yet I do not consider this young man a failure.

Why is the Christian church of today powerless? Christians should consider carefully the cause. One of the members of a labor union in Kobe pawned all his clothes and gave the money to the union, and when more was needed was ready even to sell the mats covering the floor of his house to help along the strike. When Japanese Christians become dead in earnest enough to sell off even their house mats for the sake of their religion, Christianity will have power. The churches of the present have not got as much zeal as have the labor unions.

Jesus Christ spent all he had for his movement. He said to a rich young man, "Go, sell what you own . . . then come!" Jesus seems to have been a very successful carpenter. In the apocryphal Gospels it is written that Jesus made the throne for Herod's palace. He might have become a nouveau riche if he had not given it up for a religious movement. But Jesus chose not that way to so-called success, but the road that led to poverty and to the Cross. And there he gained true success.

If you are a failure now, it is your best chance to come to Jesus. A man I know opened a trading company at the time of the war and he was almost mad with joy because he made £400,000. But when the financial panic came, he failed badly, and he had to close more than ten of the branches of his company. When I saw him about that time, he said to me, "Mr. Kagawa, a good time has come to me! I am attending church from now on!" And indeed after that he became really earnest and has been going to church ever since. So if you are involved in some sort of failure in your everyday life, in a disappointing love affair or an economic problem, it is a good opportunity for you. God takes advantage of your despair over failure. If through the power of Jesus you can rise up again, the success will compensate your failure billions of times over.

The Cost of Following Jesus

From *The Religion of Jesus*, Chapter V,
"The Relation of Jesus to His Disciples"

In this selection, Kagawa comments on what it means to give all we have, take up the cross, and follow Christ.

To be a disciple of Jesus, one needs a great resolution. It is a mistake to become a disciple of Jesus expecting to be famous or to become a religious success. It is always a road of hardship and persecution. There are occasionally some who reach success socially or become famous because they believe in a given religion, but this is never the ordinary case. If one is trampled on and considered worthless because of belief in Christianity, that person may rather be the one who walks the road of the true reconstruction of the world.

A man belonging to the intelligentsia came to Jesus and asked him to make him a disciple. But Jesus, seeing that it was hard for a man who is accustomed to reading books and living in comfort to partake in a practical movement for religious propaganda, refused decisively and said, "Foxes have holes, and birds of the air have nests; but the Son of Man has nowhere to lay his head." Also to the man who said, "First let me go and bury my father," Jesus said, "Follow me, and let the dead bury their own dead." If you do not have this resolution, you cannot be a disciple of Jesus. It may be that you will not be able to see your father on his deathbed. Christians of today are not enthusiastic enough.

Although it is not necessary to give up all economic life in order to follow Jesus, it must be admitted that there is some incompatibility between following Jesus and keeping hold of anything that belongs to the world. To follow Jesus really, you must be ready to give up the whole of your business or profession. Your business ought to become God's possession—what belongs to God. At the very least you must have the resolution to offer your life to God if God requires it. You must offer God not 10 percent but 100 percent. It is at this point that the Japanese church of today is cold and indifferent.

The wife of Juji Ishii, the founder of the Okayama Orphanage, heard once at a prayer meeting a suggestion that unless one offered to God everything, one could not be a disciple, and she recalled that she had one thing put away in a cabinet that she had thought she could not offer to God. It was a silk Obi (sash) worth about ten pounds, which her mother had woven specially for her. She had given up everything else, but could not let this one sash go out of her hand. But when she heard a voice, *"Sell what you own . . . then come, follow me,"* she sold it at last, changed it into money, and gave the money to beggars who were at the end of the bridge in the town of Okayama one cold winter night.

There are some who say that we, who must live a civilized life, need more of a taste for the arts. And that on that account we have nothing left to offer to God. But can you really follow Jesus if you remain like that? How can you say that you are a disciple of Jesus without offering your 100 percent? How can you attempt to work for true social reformation? Return Caesar's to Caesar, and humanity's to humanity. If you make money by some invention, give it all back to the people in the society that enabled you to earn. Without paying any fee we have all been admitted into a wonderful world; and if, in addition, we come into touch with the love of Jesus, how can we remain unmoved? After all, we entered the world naked, and therefore we ought to leave it in the same condition. I cannot admire a man who, while calling himself a disciple of Jesus, yet says he must have a cultured life and wants to live in luxury in a big house. For his whole life Jesus wandered from village to village, spending his life on foot, and having no place to rest. Do we not need once more to return to Jesus?

From my experience in the labor movement I know that if ten people unite, they can do a great thing. Jesus' disciples were only twelve in number, but they were able in a very short time to recover the movement of Jesus, which seemed to have ended in defeat, and to make it a real triumph. We of today must realize that we are at a historical crisis. Do we intend to bring to Japan a revolution of blood or the blessing of Jesus? If we offer our whole spirits and whole bodies to Jesus, God will certainly bless Japan.

Jesus said, "If any want to become my followers, let them deny themselves and take their cross and follow me." He said, "Follow me," four or five times in the Gospel of Mark alone. People of the world rarely say, "Follow me," very decidedly; so it is not to be wondered at that many people go astray. When we ask the scholars, they answer us only that there are such and such theories, but they do not tell us anything decidedly. But Jesus said, "Follow me." Jesus told us to follow him carrying the cross on our backs, knowing the way is a way full of pains. That is the way to God. We must follow Jesus on this solid road.

It is a mistake if you think it a gay path of flowers. It may be to look for a sick person wandering in a dark alley, to take care of a dying patient in a hospital for infectious diseases, to be a friend of people with leprosy all your life or, like Yoshinori Tokunaga, to lie in bed for sixteen years suffering from consumption and in adverse circumstances to enjoy God's blessings. You must know that Jesus' road is a dark pass through a tunnel.

Our Need for Redemption

From *Meditations on the Cross*, Chapter VI,
"The Cross as Revealed in Paul's Parables"

*In whatever he wrote, Kagawa spoke of the redeeming love of God
revealed in the Cross. In this book of meditations (published in
English in 1935), Kagawa looks at the Cross as it is presented in
scripture and as it is lived out in daily life. This selection on the
need for redemption was translated by Helen F. Topping.*

We do not realize that the Cross is the center of Christianity.
We are likely to go only so far as to think that Christ's sacrifice
makes a deep impression upon people, and is therefore pre-
cious, and that Christ is an ideal personality. The bloody agony
that renounced life itself does not come home to our hearts.
That is because our way of thinking of sin is not as deep as
Christ's. If we are living a fairly good life, we are satisfied and
have no thought of assuming responsibility for the sins of others. We are too content with living from day to day.

But merely not to do evil is to be no different from the
stones in the roadway. Better to be a block of wood than to be
self-complacent at taking care of self alone! If we are merely

avoiding sin, we do not need redemption. But when once we get to feeling, as God does, a responsibility for the sins of the whole human race, we cannot remain in idleness. Idleness and indifference in the face of this sinful world are in themselves sins. It is a sin to seek escape from the turmoil of the world by flight to the mountains.

Among the parables of Christ there is the one about the talents. The servants who had been entrusted with the five and with the two talents set the money to work and gained double, but the one-talent man simply put away what had been entrusted to him. When their master returned, he reproved this servant for not setting his money to work, and said, "If that was all you were going to do with it, why did you not at the very least put my money into a bank?" And then, "Give your talent to the five-talent man." Thus Christ taught that merely to do nothing is unpardonable.

My conscience pricks me when I am doing nothing, even when forced to rest by illness. I think to myself in shame that while there are many sick people who do a great work by writing letters, I am merely concerned with curing my own sickness! When we are content with a small life and a small measure of success, when we are content with selfish, individualistic gratification, we do not really need redemption. When we are content with such a selfish life, we cannot possibly understand how much Christ suffered for the salvation of the race.

Christ thought of sin as God does. Paul also examined himself, with a profound consciousness of his sin, and said, "The saying is sure and worthy of full acceptance, that Christ Jesus came into the world to save sinners—of whom I am the foremost." I am the captain of all criminals, he was saying remorsefully. But had he committed a great crime? He had not committed adultery. He had not stolen. He had not killed anyone with his own hands. Nevertheless he examined himself, and because he had been enlightened by God, he had a deep consciousness of sin.

Paul was rather better than the average Jew. But compared to God, compared to Christ, he had lived below the right standard. Moreover, even considering his education and ancestry, he knew he ought to have done better. So he thought of himself as the chief of sinners. When Christ had done so much for the human race, he, Paul, had misinterpreted it and had rejoiced in the killing of Christ's disciples. He was terribly ashamed of this. To be sure he had been ignorant, and so might reasonably have been forgiven. But when he examined himself, when he laid bare his faults, he realized that he must repent before God. People today have a very dull sense of sin. When they are brought to account for their own failures, they blame their circumstances in life, the economic system, or something else, and do not admit any responsibility themselves. Their ideas of the Atonement are hazy. But anyone who, like Paul, has thought seriously about their sins, cannot get along without Christ to lovingly forgive them.

Praying "Your Will Be Done"

From *Meditations on the Cross*, Chapter IX,
"The Cross and Prayer"

*In this selection, Kagawa looks at Christ's prayer in the Garden
of Gethsemane before his arrest. This passage and the next were
translated by Marion Draper.*

We see the Christlikeness of Jesus in his repeated prayer, "Your
will be done." Had he only said, "Your will be done," it would
not have been a prayer. The words, "Remove this cup from
me," make it a true prayer. It is a human prayer, and yet it
breathes a spirit of complete consecration: "If the Cross is necessary, make me, I ask you, take your way; I have no desires or
hopes of my own; if there is no other way, I accept your will
gladly." Here we see the point of struggle in Christ's experience. If he had been so far separated from human feelings as
to say merely, "O God, do as you will," it would not have been
genuinely human suffering. He is human because as One who
was to manifest God's will upon earth, he was caught in a
dilemma, and his nobility lies in the way he met this dilemma.
Herein, too, lies the greatness of our religion.

There are two ways of looking at the problem: God's way and humanity's way. According to the human viewpoint, we wish to map out our own road; but when we consider God's will, we throw aside our selfishness and become willing to follow God's path. The prayer at Gethsemane is the bond between these two. From the human standpoint, one is averse to the Cross; one does not wish to inflict death on oneself, but from God's viewpoint, this is unavoidable. To choose death seems like a self-contradiction; but when we really make up our minds to pray, there is no other prayer but this.

There are many of us Orientals who say, "It is God's will!" It is an old saying with us that everything is karma; everything is determined by fate. But that is equivalent to saying that we are not free to choose in any situation. One may be fated to commit murder or to die by starvation. There is nothing we can do about it. Christ's attitude, however, was that, as a human being, he was free to choose and he was determined to live his life to the full. He would exert himself to the utmost, and then what a man could not do must be left to the will of God. Herein lies the focal point of Christ's spiritual struggle. We must follow this same path. After we have poured out every bit of human effort possible, then we must say, "Let it be done according to God's will." This is the eternal Gethsemane.

There is a lesson for us in the fact that Jesus prayed the whole night through. In long-continued meditation we draw nearer and nearer to God until we make our petitions not for the advancement of our own interests but for the glory of God. The heavier the responsibilities one carries, the more numerous are the demands that one makes of God. The more one feels one's own responsibilities, the more deeply should one ponder the prayer of Christ in Gethsemane.

In the early days of Christianity in Japan, there came a moment of crisis in 1873 when there was a general cry for the extermination of the new faith. There were but a handful of Christians when Ibuka, Uemura, Okuno, and a group who were living in Dr. Brown's school received word from Tokyo that they would probably be killed. They thought their throats would be cut that very night. They met together and prayed earnestly, not for escape but that since they believed in the Cross, they might have the resolution to die upon it. In the midst of their prayer meeting, they received another communication that they had been pardoned. They were so full of joy, they hardly knew whether their heads were still on their shoulders or not. Our Christianity, Japan's Christianity, has come down to us from such a prayer meeting.

Someone has said that the work of atonement was accomplished in the Garden of Gethsemane rather than on the cross. There is some truth in this. According to Luke's account, Christ prayed with such earnestness that his sweat became drops of blood. When we think of this impassioned prayer, we realize that we, too, must pray with similar flaming earnestness for

Japan, for America, for China, for the whole world. Not one such petition is in vain. Prayer is bound to be heard.

I am particularly struck with the fact that Christ's prayer was not in the least for himself. If prayer has meaning only for oneself, it will not be heard. True prayer is not for oneself. If it voices the aspirations of humanity, it will be heard. There was not the slightest trace of selfishness in Christ's prayer: "If for the redemption of humankind, it is necessary that I should be killed, I am willing to go to my death." This attitude is the acme of the life of faith. To pray in this spirit is the highest type of religious consciousness. When in poverty, distress, or any sort of trouble we pray in this spirit, we gain the victory.

Christ gave up his life upon the cross the day after he prayed this earnest prayer. And there is proof that his prayer was answered, in that the people of the world have been drawn to him, and that even now a consciousness of the reality of Christ continues with us—a consciousness so deep and satisfying that it is fully adequate to our needs.

We do not have enough conviction about prayer. If we pray only a little, our prayers are answered only to that degree. If we pray much, we receive many answers. Christ's activity was founded on prayer. We must not make ourselves alone the center, but our prayers must show a sense of responsibility toward God for Japan, for Asia, for the whole world.

Completing the Work of Christ

From *Meditations on the Cross,* Chapter XVI,
"The Cross and Religious Life"

*In this selection, Kagawa looks at Paul as one who lived in the
light of the Cross.*

Christ did not die upon the cross because of some philosophical or theological theory. He poured out his love in
response to the groans of human souls. When one accepts
this work of Christ's with sincerity and simple gratitude, and
with a meek, submissive spirit, one can be saved. Where is
there in history any other who has thus sincerely grieved
over the sins of others and yearned to save them? By having a complete consciousness of sin, such a consciousness
as God has, he brought salvation to perfection. One who
does not consciously share this redemptive purpose of God
cannot imagine one's responsibility toward God. We are
always running away. Our consciences give us no rest when
we realize that we ought to shoulder our responsibility to the
uttermost. It is Christ alone who in all the world thought
the thing through, and then said, "I will take it all upon

myself. I will take all the responsibility for all sin upon my own shoulders."

Here is a heroic conscience! We hear all sorts of stories of troubled conscience. Is there any true comfort that we can offer other than this: "The blood of Christ, by God's grace, will atone for all your sins"? There has never been another in all history except Christ who brought to its consummate perfection the love that proposes to save others.

Christ's disciples did not understand the meaning of the Atonement at all. It was not until Paul appeared that it was understood, and by Paul only with difficulty. Paul was at first very much opposed to Christ. He thought it disgraceful to worship in such superstitious fashion the carpenter Jesus, a political revolutionary. He opposed the new cult in brave fashion, combing every corner of the country in order to persecute its believers. But no matter how bitterly Paul fought it, Christ's teaching continued to spread. As there were continually those from among his own friends who were becoming Christians, he gradually became uneasy about his own actions. And then one day, as he was walking along a road, with his heart full of uncertainty, a vision of Christ appeared to him, and he heard a voice in his ear: "Saul, Saul, why do you persecute me?" When Paul asked, "Who are you?" he was told, "I am Jesus, whom you are persecuting." He was unable to see for three days and three nights, and only when something like scales fell from his eyes was he at length able to see again.

I have had a similar experience. At one time I was unable to see for forty-five days, and a scale-like substance was removed from my eyes.

Through that experience Paul realized that the Cross of Christ was lifted up for the sake of manifesting the redemptive love of God. That was why Christ died. Sin is death. When we become the slaves of sin, we lose our strength. We are sold as slaves. Or our development is arrested; we become depraved. We wander from the way. We miss the mark. Because we have broken the law, we must have the sentence, "not guilty; set at liberty," pronounced upon us. By the Cross we are released from slavery and given freedom. We return again to life and become heirs of God. Having grasped the fact that Christ died in order to save us, we realize that we are, each one of us, the very chief of sinners, that we are such criminals as to have repaid God's mercy with enmity.

In that way Paul entered into the feelings of Christ. It was his purpose to take up for himself the work of Christ and to carry it on and to complete in time the sufferings of Christ that were lacking. Not satisfied with his own redemption, he began to work for even the material salvation of others. Individualistic religion was not enough for him, and he became an expert in helping and evangelizing the poor. In the seventh and eighth chapters of Second Corinthians, we see how he loved the poor and that it was his plan to give them aid. But he was misunderstood when he tried to do others that kindness, and all sorts of things were said about him. Nevertheless, all his life long he was a self-supporting evangelist. It was when he had gone to Jerusalem to take a gift of money for the poor that he was finally taken prisoner.

It is impossible to restrict the gospel of Christ to narrow limits. It redeems the sins of the past, restores the present, and stimulates development in the future. Moreover, this is not merely for the individual but for society as well. We must conceive of it as the liberation of the entire human race. The gospel is the message of a year of jubilee, of a year of rejoicing. It should mean the liberation—economically, politically, socially, physiologically, and spiritually—of the human race. It must mean the true emancipation of the whole of humanity.

There is a tendency to make the gospel into an innocuous, noncommittal sort of thing. But we should make it thoroughgoing and complete salvation to those who are in prison, to the poor, to those who are weakened by illness, to the unemployed. We must not think of Christ's blood as shed for the sake of the individual. We must not believe in a salvation for oneself alone, a salvation of selfish advantage, drawing water off to one's own rice fields. The salvation of the whole human race and the whole of society must be our goal.

The Spirit of Truth

From *Meditations on the Holy Spirit*, Chapter I,
"The Holy Spirit Promised by Christ"

These meditations on biblical passages concerning the Holy Spirit were published in English in 1939. The translator, Dr. Charles Logan, was the missionary whom Kagawa first heard preaching about Christ in 1903. This selection speaks of the Holy Spirit enabling people to see the universe as God sees it.

Until one has a clear consciousness of the Holy Spirit, one's religious life is a faltering victory. Receiving him, even a person like Peter suddenly becomes strong. Before that, Peter had denied Christ; but after he received the Holy Spirit, he influenced thousands of people. So this is not a small gift, but a special Spirit. The Holy Spirit is not the mere power of God. By receiving him, one enters into the life of God. Through him, one stands in the position of God and revises one's thoughts about everything. Therefore he is called the truth. The Spirit of truth referred to here is an absolute person. It is not truth such as one knows in botany, zoology, mathematics, or natural history. Before receiving the Spirit, one is accustomed to think relatively, comparing one person with another; afterward one thinks from God's standpoint. Those who have really become Christians do not merely believe in God, but think of the work of God, and with the feelings of God think of God's universe.

Those who have received the Holy Spirit come to have the feelings of God. They look anew at the history of the world. They reconsider the universe. And for the first time they come to understand the Spirit of truth who is promised in the Bible. Many feel hesitant about this and say that they cannot think of such a thing; but Christ thought in such a way: "This is the Spirit of truth, whom the world cannot receive, because it neither sees him nor knows him. You know him, because he abides with you, and he will be in you." Even though Christ thought thus, the world could not understand it. And those who live only in a material way can never receive him, see him, or know him. So it ought to be. Those who live only in a relative way can never think of the work of God.

Some people think that when one receives the Holy Spirit, special changes take place. That may be one result; but the Holy Spirit himself, having the mind of God, enables a person to see the truth anew. Those who come that far are different from the relative world. They guide others from the material world to the standpoint of the Absolute, thus leading others to see humankind from God's point of view: "You know him, because he abides with you, and he will be in you."

For this reason, from now on, they can do their duty toward others; and their prayer life bubbles up. When prayer springs up, they have the desire to save others. Furthermore, they would make amends for the failures of others. It is then that they understand the mind of Christ and comprehend him: "I have said these things to you while I am still with you. But the Advocate, the Holy Spirit, whom the Father will send in my name, will teach you everything, and remind you of all that I have said to you." Until one has the mind of God, one does not understand Christ.

It is when we have decided to enter into this absolute life and to have the mind of God that we come to understand truly the death of Christ. Niitaka Mountain in Formosa [Taiwan] is back of high mountains so that its summit cannot be seen from the base. So it is with Christ. When we enter the inner heart of the Absolute God, when we share the feelings of the Holy Spirit, when we are lifted up almost to the feelings of Christ, then we come to understand how much the Absolute God suffers for people, and how much Christ works and suffers for humankind. Then for the first time, we are able to comprehend everything that Christ did, to nod our heads in assent, and to understand why he did this and why he did that.

But we must not think that this is an unconscious dreamy feeling. When we see everything with the mind of God, we come to understand that the words "in my name" mean belief in the true existence of Christ, and mean, like Christ, having a heart that would try to love the universe with the feeling of God. Unless we come to have a mind that would make amends for every part of the failings of us all, we cannot understand Christ.

The Holy Spirit in Us

From *Meditations on the Holy Spirit,* Chapter VI,
"The Holy Spirit Dwelling in Man"

*In this selection Kagawa insists that religion which is not based
on experience of the Spirit is "not a real thing." He has been talk-
ing about amazement at the wonders of nature as a first step in
religion.*

But when we proceed one step beyond this feeling of wonder,
we come to feel that we are living in God and God in us. This
experience, I think, is the vital experience of the Holy Spirit.
Paul said, "It is no longer I who live, but it is Christ who lives in
me." The presence of the great God of heaven and earth is moving within us. We are borrowed things. When we live in God,
we feel that we are separated from the world; but as we feel the
mission of having God reveal the divine presence in our lim-
ited, vile bodies, we have the experience of God taking possession of these ugly, despicable bodies. God possesses us. It is the
experience of God living in us rather than of us living in God.

This experience is revealed in the Scriptures as the experience of the Holy Spirit. Without this experience of the Holy

Spirit, religion is not a real thing. And it has not fundamentally come to us. We must have a religion in which God comes near to us and in which, one step farther, all of daily life is permeated with God's presence. Eating and drinking and conducting family affairs, we must so live as to find the joy of being immersed completely in God—in God's beauty and joy and nobility and majesty. In that place there is no fear, and we are not frightened by people. This is the experience of the Holy Spirit.

When we advance this far, the first thing to well up in us is joy. Jesus Christ said, "I will not leave you orphaned." He said, "God is your Father." He would not treat God and people differently. He did not speak of people and the transcendent God as separated. He did not teach that God is far off and to be feared. He did not teach that God had cast us off. Always God is the Comforter. God would have us feel that we are embraced in warm cotton.

When we realize this, Christ is the truth. He is truth so clear that we can see through to the bottom of the sea. When my eyes are bad, it seems that my eyeglasses are dim. The water is clear; but when my eyes are bad, I cannot see the bottom. I cannot distinguish between water and land. As my eyes get better, I can gradually see. When we brighten our souls in regard to God, it is like that. When we have experience of God, and live in God, our souls become clear; and then the universe becomes clear. When our hearts become clear, back of all things we find there is the plan of God. Ancient people called that *Komyo-Henjo,* or illumination. Until we have this experience, religion is foolishness. When we have this feeling of illumination, we overcome whatever temptation we may have. Just as when we have really learned English, we do not forget it; so when we have once entered into this experience of illumination, we cannot live a muddy life, even if we would.

Paul spoke of that experience in the words, "It is Christ who lives in me," and "That very Spirit intercedes with sighs too deep for words." God lives in us. Paul clearly understood the feeling expressed in the words, "He is in all things." In the Western world people came to have this religious experience after Christianity became prevalent. And they had it in a remarkable way after the Middle Ages. Meister Eckhart and Tauler in the Middle Ages tasted the joy of the indwelling of God. It resulted in the movement of the Middle Ages to perfect people while on earth. Up to that time in the presence of the transcendent God, people were like the dust of the earth and had a feeling of helplessness and despair.

The thing that brought about the revival movements that extended from the Middle Ages down to modern times was the thought that a superhuman Power is working upon us, rather than the thought of us offering something to God. This brought about the revival of Protestantism. But even so, God was considered as one to be feared, and as only a Judge who must exercise dreadful judgment upon us. For example, men like Calvin taught that God was to be feared, and that God was a God of judgment. Sooner or later we must appear before God, so there was a feeling of despair. That feeling prevailed through the eighteenth century.

Then there came the revival movements at the close of the eighteenth century that proclaimed human perfection through the experience of God, when the power of God is added to our power. That brought about the Methodists. Consequently, there were those who, while praying according to the Lord's Prayer, "Your kingdom come. Your will be done, on earth as it is in heaven," (Matt. 6:10) desired to build the kingdom of God on earth, and who, while having the experience of the Holy Spirit, began the labor movement, and social movements, and world evangelism, and the preaching of the gospel to savage peoples. They taught that this wonderful experience of living in God should become the foundation of the new civilization. But though they taught this experience to others, many of them did not experience it. Such people as Wesley and John Fletcher had a deep experience of it. But as their teaching yielded to the spirit of culture and civilization, it became muddy and indistinct, and lost its power.

Full Consciousness

From *Meditations on the Holy Spirit,* Chapter VII,
"The Holy Spirit as Truth"

In many of his writings, Kagawa contrasts those who are conscious only of the natural world (the "semiconscious") and those who, through the Spirit, have become "fully conscious." Here is an excellent short statement of this idea.

If we have the feelings of the God of the universe, even though we have been placed in beautiful surroundings, we will not forget the proletarians. We can have the will of Christ to comfort the lonely. Semiconscious love is a natural love, like the love of sweethearts, or the love of parents and children. It is the relation of part to part. Therefore semiconscious love, even though it is 70 percent conscious, is not a love of the whole consciousness. Mutual love is also so. But when there is a love of the whole consciousness, it wants to save even those who are opposed to one. And an ethical love does not produce an atoning love. Therefore a love of the entire consciousness is of the consciousness of Christ. When the consciousness of Christ has come into us, that is the consciousness of the Holy Spirit.

When we receive the Holy Spirit, the first result is an outflow of prayer. Prayer does not flow out of us without the Holy Spirit. What is the difference between prayer and desire? Desire is like a child asking his or her mother for candy or a toy. Prayer is looking up to the mind of the God of the universe and, making God's will the foundation, asking for things. The reason why people in modern times do not pray is that they cannot come to have the feelings of God. There are many proletarians in the world. If we have a desire to help them, then we can pray. To God, who has a duty even to the poor who have no property, our prayers flow forth. That is true prayer.

And when we have the will of Christ, there is an outflow of prayer. True prayer is to have the feelings of God. It is for those who have disabilities, whether physical or mental or moral or economic or ethical, to come to have the feelings of God and pray. When the Holy Spirit begins to work in us, we cannot keep from praying. And it becomes prayer "in the name of Christ." Unless we have a consciousness like that of Christ, true prayer does not spring up in our hearts. It is most important that we pray believing in the fact of the love of Christ.

Next is given sanctification. If we enter into a condition of full consciousness, all our sins melt away. For example, all those things that are forbidden in the Ten Commandments, such as disobedience, murder, adultery, stealing, lying, and avarice, cannot be done when we have entered into full consciousness.

As for the attitude of children to their parents, when the children have the feelings of God, even though the parents may be in the wrong, as they themselves must save their parents, there is no room for disobedience to them. Murderers, too, when they come to full consciousness, feel that they must help others, and they cannot kill. As for adultery, too, even though the wife is old, she is a part of a man's self; so even if she is in the wrong, a man must bring back that part of himself to do right. If they were separate parts, they might separate; but when one thinks of the whole, there can be no divorce. That is the reason there can be no adultery. And again, when one thinks of the whole, one cannot steal; for it is like stealing one's own things. And lying would be like lying to oneself. And avarice would be the same. Therefore when we come into full consciousness, into the consciousness of Christ, we enter forever into perfect sanctification. That is sanctification through the Holy Spirit.

When we look at it from the standpoint of a fully conscious love, through the Holy Spirit, we know that the cross of Christ is an atoning love. He who shows this to us is the Spirit of truth. The awakening from the natural instincts to a full consciousness is the truth.

However, there is an order in this, just as trees grow. By those who are infants, this Holy Spirit is not understood. But when God's universal consciousness is transmitted to us, we can understand. Unless we come to feel that we would assume all the troubles of tenants, and proletarians, and fishermen, and laborers in the cities, there is no outflow of prayer. The Holy Spirit is given because we pray. When we come into the consciousness of the Holy Spirit, and come to have a conviction, a religious life becomes very pleasant. Even though there are hardships, they are nothing. For that reason the Holy Spirit is called the Advocate, the Comforter.

Such a religious experience has appeared throughout the long history of the Christian church. In the movements of love in the Christian church, this Holy Spirit is certainly engaged. We must stop hunting heresy with a cold attitude, separate ourselves from a self-centered, self-satisfied church life, enter into a consciousness of the Cross to save sinners, and enter into this blessed life filled with the Holy Spirit. When we look at nature from a holy life, nature seems to shine with light. I think this is the reason that Paul asked people if they had received the Holy Spirit. It is not mere repentance. Repentance cannot bring us to full consciousness. It is not sufficient. We must weave this Holy Spirit into our daily living. That is, the Holy Spirit is the truth of God, the truth of Christ, the truth of humankind, the truth of conscience, and gives us consciousness from within. This full consciousness of the truth itself is the greatest gift that God has promised to people.

Joy in the Spirit

From *Meditations on the Holy Spirit,* Chapter VIII,
"The Holy Spirit as Comforter"

The Spirit brings us to full knowledge of how we are loved by God.
One result of that knowledge is joy.

If the religion of Christ had not worked for the poor of the first century of Rome, giving the experience of the Holy Spirit, human history would not be such as it is today. The religion of love, which anyone, however poor, could experience and thereby enter into the consciousness of the children of God, which taught that God and human become one in Christ, changed the history of the world. Yes, through the reception of the Holy Spirit, even the most insignificant of people could enter for the first time into joy of fellowship with God.

The experience of the indwelling of the Holy Spirit has a threefold joy. First is the realization that the sins of the past are all forgiven through the blood of Christ. Second is the consciousness that we who are already forgiven are kept by God, and that without fear we may draw near to God, and that we may joyfully live with God in a life of prayer. And third is the conviction that positively we may bear the cross, and that from the standpoint of the love of God we may become useful for the salvation of sinners.

Experiencing this joy, Paul spoke of himself, "I am now rejoicing in my sufferings for your sake, and in my flesh I am completing what is lacking in Christ's afflictions for the sake of his body, that is, the church." And to the Philippians, he wrote, "For he has graciously granted you the privilege not only of believing in Christ, but of suffering for him as well." On examining the thirteen epistles of Paul, one finds that at first he was despondent about sin, but that after he became a prisoner and lived in prison, even though in prison, he could taste the life of the Holy Spirit and was filled with joy, so that in his letter to the Philippians he repeated the word *joy* more than ten times. On account of his understanding of the life of the Holy Spirit he lived a fruitful life filled with hope.

In this way, by the Holy Spirit, truth was revealed to Paul. By the Holy Spirit love was poured upon him. Believing that a courageous will had been given to him, he felt very happy. He felt his duty to those in trouble, and as he felt this joy he knew that nothing could harm him. He understood that this joy first arose in human consciousness by the indwelling of God, and that God who sustained him from within was the Comforter.

Through the consciousness of the presence of the indwelling Comforter, life is changed. Death and trouble and persecution are no longer problems to be considered. The joy of the presence of God's Spirit cannot be interpreted by reason. Many Christians really experience this. By the Holy Spirit, we can easily pass through death.

Really, there are no words to express the experience of the Holy Spirit. I have felt such religious joy several times, and I have had the joy of being immersed in light; there are no words to describe that joy. I have felt an absolute joy that cannot be tasted in such pleasures as fame or gain or the pleasures of the physical nature.

Christ said, "Receive the Holy Spirit"; and at once he added, "If you forgive the sins of any, they are forgiven." That means the same as when he said "Abide in my love." That is, the Holy Spirit, as the truth, gives the content of consciousness. As the Sanctifier, he gives a guarantee of our perfection. But that again is not separate from his atoning love. The realization of this love is altogether by the power of the Holy Spirit. Paul who experienced this love received the power to overcome all things with the joy of love.

Really, the Holy Spirit and love cannot be separated. Christ came into the world to show to the human race the love of God. All the teachings of Christ have relation to this love. Salvation means that God is love. Providence also means that we are kept by the love of God. Judgment means that God will weed out those who do not believe in the love of God. God is love. Christ is the crystal of God's love. The Holy Spirit is the Spirit of truth who reveals the atoning love of Christ.

This love is not the love that the world gives. It is the love that God gives. The love of the world is semiconscious. It loves only those whom it likes. But the love that is the fruit of the Holy Spirit is the full, conscious, atoning love that loves even those whom it dislikes.

When we thus think, all the teaching of Christ is love. Through the consciousness of the joy of this love, it flows out eternally like never-ceasing oil from a vessel. It is at this point the evangelist John says that the Holy Spirit and love are not to be separated. The mystical experience of the Holy Spirit is the intuitive recognition of the love of God. For that reason, those who have had a deep experience of the Holy Spirit, however poor they may be, whatever sickness they may suffer, however much they may be persecuted, rejoice in the unceasing love of God. Truly, in this meaning, the Holy Spirit is the Comforter, and we may say he is our Helper. The religion of the love of Christ is not a religion of fear. It is the fountain of love and joy and life. We must live forever in his love.

Love

From *Songs from the Slums*

Here, in a nutshell, is Kagawa's understanding of the Christian life.

My God is Love;
My God is Love,
Tender and deep;
I feel His close, sweet presence
Looking down to see
The beggar-baby
Lying in my arms asleep.

Appendix

*Reading Spiritual Classics for Personal
and Group Formation*

Many Christians today are searching for more spiritual depth, for something more than simply being good church members. That quest may send them to the spiritual practices of New Age movements or of Eastern religions such as Zen Buddhism. Christians, though, have their own long spiritual tradition, a tradition rich with wisdom, variety, and depth.

The great spiritual classics testify to that depth. They do not concern themselves with mystical flights for a spiritual elite. Rather, they contain very practical advice and insights that can support and shape the spiritual growth of any Christian. We can all benefit by sitting at the feet of the masters (both male and female) of Christian spirituality.

Reading spiritual classics is different from most of the reading we do. We have learned to read to master a text and extract information from it. We tend to read quickly, to get through a text. And we summarize as we read, seeking the main point. In reading spiritual classics, though, we allow the text to master and form us. Such formative reading goes more slowly, more reflectively, allowing time for God to speak to us through the text. God's word for us may come as easily from a minor point or even an aside as from the major point.

Formative reading requires that you approach the text in humility. Read as a seeker, not an expert. Don't demand that the text meet your expectations for what an "enlightened" author should write. Humility means accepting the author as another imperfect human, a product of his or her own time and situation. Learn to celebrate what is foundational in an author's writing without being overly disturbed by what is peculiar to the author's life and times. Trust the text as a gift from both God and the author, offered to you for your benefit—to help you grow in Christ.

To read formatively, you must also slow down. Feel free to reread a passage that seems to speak specially to you. Stop from time to time to reflect on what you have been reading. Keep a journal for these reflections. Often the act of writing can itself prompt further, deeper reflection. Keep your notebook open and your pencil in hand as you read. You might not get back to that wonderful insight later. Don't worry that you are not getting through an entire passage—or even the first paragraph! Formative reading is about depth rather than breadth, quality rather than quantity. As you read, seek God's direction for your own life. Timeless truths have their place but may not be what is most important for your own formation here and now.

As you read the passage, you might keep some of these questions running through your mind:

- How is what I'm reading true of my own life? Where does it reflect my own *experience*?
- How does this text challenge me? What new *direction* does it offer me?
- What must I change to put what I am reading into practice? How can I *incarnate* it, let this word become flesh in my life?

You might also devote special attention to sections that upset you. What is the source of the disturbance? Do you want to argue theology? Are you turned off by cultural differences? Or have you been skewered by an insight that would turn your life upside down if you took it seriously? Let your journal be a dialogue with the text.

If you find yourself moving from reading the text to chewing over its implications to praying, that's great! Spiritual reading is really the first step in an ancient way of prayer called *lectio divina* or "divine reading." Reading leads naturally into reflection on what you have read (meditation). As you reflect on what the text might mean for your life, you may well want to ask for God's help in living out any new insights or direction you have perceived (prayer). Sometimes such prayer may lead you further into silently abiding in God's presence (contemplation). And, of course, the process is only really completed when it begins to make a difference in the way we live (incarnation).

As good as it is to read spiritual classics in solitude, it is even better to join with others in a small group for mutual formation or "spiritual direction in common." This is *not* the same as a study group that talks about spiritual classics. A group for mutual formation would have similar goals as for an individual's reading: to allow the text to shine its light on the *experiences* of the group members, to suggest new *directions* for their lives and practical ways of *incarnating* these directions. Such a group might agree to focus on one short passage from a classic at each meeting (even if members have read more). Discussion usually goes much deeper if all the members have already read and reflected on the passage before the meeting and bring their journals.

Such groups need to watch for several potential problems. It is easy to go off on a tangent (especially if it takes the focus off the members' own experience and onto generalities). At such times a group leader might bring the group's attention back to the text: "What does our author say about that?" Or, "How do we experience that in our own lives?" When a group member shares a problem, others may be tempted to try to "fix" it. This is much less helpful than sharing similar experiences and how they were handled (for good or ill). "Sharing" someone else's problems (whether that person is in or out of the group) should be strongly discouraged.

One person could be designated as leader, to be responsible for opening and closing prayers; to be the first to share or respond to the text; and to keep notes during the discussion to highlight recurring themes, challenges, directives, or practical steps. These responsibilities could also be shared among several members of the group or rotated.

For further information about formative reading of spiritual classics, try *A Practical Guide to Spiritual Reading* by Susan Annette Muto. *Shaped by the Word: The Power of Scripture in Spiritual Formation* by M. Robert Mulholland Jr. covers formative reading of the Bible. *Good Things Happen: Experiencing Community in Small Groups* by Dick Westley is an excellent resource on forming small groups of all kinds.

CPSIA information can be obtained
at www.ICGtesting.com
Printed in the USA
FSOW02n2200070317
31653FS